African Animals
Reptiles
Monkeys
Birds

Creature Features

Maria Valdez

Illustrated by Jeff Lang

"Welcome!" said Zelda. "Let's tour the zoo.
Try to answer each question.
I'll give you a clue."

African Animals

Monkeys

SHO

welcome

3

"I'll show you an animal that can be hard to see. It has a long body. What can it be?"

Reptiles

4

"It's a snake!" we said.

6

"I'll show you an animal that's as tall as a tree. It has a long neck. What can it be?"

"It's a giraffe!" we said.

"I'll show you an animal that swims in the sea. It has webbed feet. What can it be?"

"It's a penguin!" we said.

"I'll show you an animal that swings in a tree. It has a long tail. What can it be?"

11

"It's a monkey!" we said.

12

"I'll show you an animal that can fly over me. It has a white head. What can it be?"

"It's an eagle!" we said.

14

"Yes, here at the zoo we have lots of creatures.
All of them have amazing features!"

"Thank you!" we said. "We had a great time.
We learned so much from each animal rhyme."

Exit